MILAN
THE CITY AT A GLANCE

MW00469170

Torre Velasca
Equally admired and criticised, the
unusual design of the Torre Velasca pays a
backhanded compliment to the city's castle.
See p011

Castello Sforzesco
The once-foreboding epicentre of Milan's
medieval power now welcomes allcomers
to its museums and manicured courtyards.
Piazza Castello

Duomo
It's the sheer scale of the city's 14th-century
cathedral, adorned with 500 years of marble
statuary, that stops visitors in their tracks.
See p014

Torre Unicredit
The most distinctive peak in a new, improved
skyline does the twist in Porta Nuova.
See p010

Torre Solaria
This 143m three-pronged residential block by
Miami firm Arquitectonica is festooned with
balconies to take advantage of the fine views.
Viale della Liberazione 2-16

Torre Breda
Luigi Mattioni's 1954 tower maintained the
quaint custom of not surpassing the height of
the Duomo's Madonna statue. Such reverence
held no truck with Gio Ponti four years later.
Piazza della Repubblica

Pirelli Tower
Ponti's 'Pirellone' is a beloved symbol of the
postwar boom years when modern design
took bold strides forward. He went big, too.
See p013

INTRODUCTION

THE CHANGING FACE OF THE URBAN SCENE

Depending on your perspective, Milan is either located in the south of northern Europe, or in the north of the south, which is why the Milanese, with their proximity to Switzerland, Austria and France, feel closer to the continent than the peninsula. A city of fast-paced industry, work and progress, it is often claimed that Milan is not as animated by food, family or free time as the rest of Italy (whether this is true is contentious), but it does align itself with the business capitals of Europe. After the flurry of development for Expo 2015, it hopes to prove it belongs in this club – and deserves to remain. The clusters of new skyscrapers with sustainable engineering designed by global architects certainly lend it a more refined air.

Unlike Rome, Venice or Florence, Milan doesn't offer up its finest wares on a plate, so you'll have to work harder to uncover its gems. Many visitors come for the annual events, including Fashion Week and the highly influential furniture show Salone del Mobile in April when the city is transformed, as any available space is turned into a showroom. Others are drawn by the retail – there's no better place to shop, as the most enticing boutiques are close together and sell limited editions that are not to be found elsewhere. The original beacon of luxury is the 150-year-old <u>Galleria Vittorio Emanuele II</u> (see p080), its frescoes and decor now fully restored – in Milan, a proper entrance and a *bella figura* are paramount. This is, after all, a city fixated by style, where looking your best is a way of life.

ESSENTIAL INFO
FACTS, FIGURES AND USEFUL ADDRESSES

TOURIST OFFICE
Piazza Castello 1
T 02 7740 4343
www.turismo.milano.it

TRANSPORT
Airport transfer to city centre
Urban Line 73 departs Linate Airport
every 10 minutes from 5.35am to 12.35am
(€1.50). Malpensa Express departs to
Cadorna or Central Station every 30
minutes from 5.25am to 1.30am (€12)
Car hire
Avis
T 02 8901 0645
Metro
www.atm-mi.it
Trains run daily, from 6am to 12.30am. A
weekly unlimited travel card costs €11.30
(reusable card must be bought: €10)
Taxis
Radio Taxi
T 02 8585
Find cabs at ranks or book one in advance

EMERGENCY SERVICES
Ambulance
T 118
Fire
T 115
Police
T 113
Late-night pharmacy
Stazione Centrale Farmacie
Galleria della Partenze
T 02 669 0735

CONSULATES
British Consulate-General
Via San Paolo 7
T 06 4220 2431
www.gov.uk/government/world/italy

US Consulate-General
Via Principe Amedeo 2-10
T 02 290 351
milan.usconsulate.gov

POSTAL SERVICES
Post office
Via Cordusio 4
T 02 7248 2126
Shipping
Mail Boxes Etc
T 02 6762 5544

BOOKS
A Traveller in Italy by HV Morton
(Da Capo Press)
Gio Ponti by Ugo La Pietra
(Rizzoli International Publications)

WEBSITES
Art/Design
www.thatscontemporary.com
Newspaper
www.corriere.it

EVENTS
Cortili Aperti
www.adsi.it
Salone Internazionale del Mobile
www.cosmit.it

COST OF LIVING
Taxi from Linate Airport to city centre
€25
Cappuccino
€1.70
Packet of cigarettes
€5
Daily newspaper
€1.50
Bottle of champagne
€70

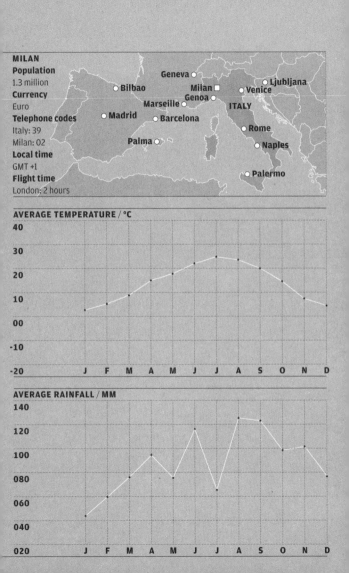

MILAN

Population
1.3 million

Currency
Euro

Telephone codes
Italy: 39
Milan: 02

Local time
GMT +1

Flight time
London: 2 hours

Geneva
Bilbao
Milan □
Ljubljana
Venice
Madrid
Marseille
Genoa
ITALY
Barcelona
Rome
Palma
Naples
Palermo

AVERAGE TEMPERATURE / °C

40												
30												
20												
10												
00												
-10												
-20	J	F	M	A	M	J	J	A	S	O	N	D

AVERAGE RAINFALL / MM

140												
120												
100												
080												
060												
040												
020	J	F	M	A	M	J	J	A	S	O	N	D

NEIGHBOURHOODS
THE AREAS YOU NEED TO KNOW AND WHY

To help you navigate the city, we've chosen the most interesting districts (see below and the map inside the back cover) and colour-coded our featured venues, according to their location; those venues that are outside these areas are not coloured.

MAGENTA

The oldest *pasticceria* in Milan, and still one of the finest, Pasticceria Marchesi (see p024) is just down the road from the convent of Santa Maria delle Grazie, where the star attraction is Leonardo da Vinci's *The Last Supper*. To the east, by Sempione, visit Museo Archeologico (Corso Magenta 15, T 02 8844 5208) for its architecture and ancient artefacts. Over in the west, unorthodox design gallery Spazio Rossana Orlandi (see p068) showcases new talent.

SEMPIONE

Expo Gate frames Castello Sforzesco (see p054) and its museums. Beyond its moat is Parco Sempione, dotted with architectural gems including the Triennale (see p025), the Liberty-style Acquario (Viale Gadio 2), built for the 1906 Expo, and the ornate 1838 Arco della Pace, designed by Luigi Cagnola to celebrate Napoleon's victories. The arch faces Paris, and these days the chintzy bars lining Corso Sempione.

ZONA DUOMO/CENTRO

The Duomo (see p014) stands at the heart of the city, flanked by the magnificent 19th-century arcade Galleria Vittorio Emanuele II, which leads to Piazza della Scala, and by the Palazzo Reale, the medieval seat of government now host to some of the city's most significant art exhibits. Adjacent is the Museo del Novecento (see p078), with masterpieces by Umberto Boccioni, Giorgio de Chirico and Carla Accardi among others.

QUADRILATERO DELLA MODA

Milan's famed 'Golden Triangle' is a dense concentration of luxury boutiques. The high demand for space has led to overflow into Montenapoleone, invading Via Verri, San Pietro all'Orto and Corso Venezia too. The district encompasses such emblems of good taste as collectors' haven Nilufar (see p091) and the timeless fashion of Aspesi (see p088), as well as a jewel-box historic house museum, the Bagatti Valsecchi (Via Gesù 5, T 02 7600 6132).

BRERA

The old artists' quarter behind the late 18th-century opera house La Scala (Via Filodrammatici 2, T 02 88 791) is now filled with design galleries, upscale shops and a flourishing restaurant scene, with Pisacco (Via Solferino 48, T 02 9176 5472) and Dry (see p031) injecting new energy. Pinacoteca di Brera (see p054) boasts a prestigious collection of Renaissance art, and a lovely, peaceful botanical garden.

NAVIGLI/ZONA TORTONA

Most of Milan's main arteries were former waterways, and the city's remaining canals form the axes of nightlife in charming Navigli, from the converted warehouses of Tortona — now colonised by designers and architects — to the Roman columns of San Lorenzo. Smart venues like Turbigo (see p040) and Rebelot (Ripa di Porta Ticinese 55, T 02 8419 4720) offer sophisticated concepts among the happy-hour bars.

LANDMARKS

THE SHAPE OF THE CITY SKYLINE

Milan's historic centre winds around the Duomo (see p014), from where arteries radiate out to the ring roads. To the north is the monumental 1931 Stazione Centrale (Piazza Duca d'Aosta 1) and the transformed Porta Nuova district, which has added diversity to the topography once dominated by Gio Ponti's iconic statement for Pirelli (see p013). Here, in the former 'squatters' village', Torre Unicredit (overleaf) spirals to the city's highest point, close to the 161m Palazzo Lombardia (Piazza Città di Lombardia 1) and Kohn Pedersen Fox's soaring Torre Diamante (Viale Della Liberazione), all linked by a landscaped promenade to Bosco Verticale (see p073).

Considerable effort was expended to add a cosmopolitan sheen for Expo. The original Fiera district to the west is now also home to the clunkily named CityLife, due for completion in 2018, which is being populated with towers by Arata Isozaki, Zaha Hadid and Daniel Libeskind. To the south, the ancient 'Little Port' of Darsena has undergone a facelift, with a park built over the water, leading to the two remaining Navigli canals and the creative community of Tortona. Then all the warehouses give way to fields of rice and corn, and to Lombardy's 18th-century farmhouses, many of which have been restructured as public spaces to tie in with the agrarian theme of Expo. Yet despite all this urban development and the fast-rising skyline, on a smog-free day it is the Alps that still dominate. *For full addresses, see Resources.*

Torre Unicredit

The most dramatic statement in the vast overhaul of Porta Nuova, Torre Unicredit is Italy's tallest building, thanks to an 84m corkscrew spire, illuminated at night, that takes its total height to 217.7m. Designed by architects Pelli Clarke Pelli and opened in 2012, the 31-storey asymmetrical tower and its two smaller neighbours – standing at 100m and 61.5m – are clad in reflective glass. The three slim, curved forms, linked at the base by a glass-and-steel canopy atop retail space, encircle Piazza Gae Aulenti, where a 'dancing fountain' covers the slate square with a veil of water and Alberto Garutti's interactive *Egg* sculpture comprises 23 brass tubes that link various levels down to the underground car park. The audio installation reverberates with snatched conversation and ambient noise. *Piazza Gae Aulenti*

Torre Velasca

Much debated at home and abroad at the time of its construction, the 1958 Torre Velasca was designed by BBPR (Gian Luigi Banfi, Lodovico Barbiano di Belgiojoso, Enrico Peressutti and Ernesto Nathan Rogers). A remarkable take on a medieval fortress, it swells at the residential upper storeys, resembling a watchtower, and its cantilevered supports are an inverted nod to the Duomo's famous buttresses

(see p014). The spacing of the windows is irregular, creating an interesting dynamic to the facade. The lobby is the only part of the building open to the public – after a stroll in the surrounding plaza, visit the nearby Rotonda della Besana (Via Besana 12), a deconsecrated late baroque church with an unusual curving colonnade, now host to cultural events and a garden bistro.
Piazza Velasca 5

Torre Branca

Next door to the Triennale di Milano design museum (see p025), Torre Branca is an elegant metal tower looming 108m above Parco Sempione. It was designed by Gio Ponti with Cesare Chiodi and Ettore Ferrari in 1933 for the fifth Triennale (exhibitions were previously held once every three years, hence the name). For €5 you can ride up to the viewing platform, although you'll need a head for heights and a fair degree of patience as the lift carries only seven people at a time and visitors have to descend before the next lot are allowed up. Opening hours can also be erratic, so call ahead, but it is worth the hassle for such a rewarding panorama. Pop into the flamboyant Just Cavalli bar (T 02 311 817) at the base to calm the nerves afterwards. *Viale Luigi Camoens 2, Parco Sempione, T 02 331 4120*

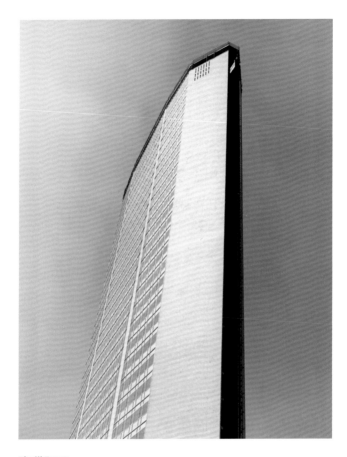

Pirelli Tower

This iconic skyscraper near the Stazione Centrale is proof positive that a modernist high-rise need not result in repetitive banality. Constructed for tyre giant Pirelli and completed in 1958, it was the tallest building in the country, at 127m, until it was overshadowed by Pei Cobb Freed & Partners' Palazzo Lombardia (see p009) in 2010. Its architect, Gio Ponti, was joined by several collaborators on the project, including engineer Pier Luigi Nervi, and the design helped shape Ponti's career. In 1978, unable to meet the tower's huge running costs, Pirelli sold it to the local government, which, despite relocating to Palazzo Lombardia in 2011, retains some office space here. Il Pirellone, as it's fondly known, was completely refurbished after a small plane famously flew into it in 2002. *Piazza Duca d'Aosta 3*

Duomo

Although it was commissioned in 1386, the world's fourth-largest cathedral was only completed in the mid-1800s. It's a startling confection of white Candoglia marble, with 135 spires and thousands of statues — a motley crew of characters best viewed face-to-face from the roof. Restoration of the fragile stone is never-ending; the facade was scoured for 2015.

Piazza del Duomo

HOTELS

WHERE TO STAY AND WHICH ROOMS TO BOOK

Milan lacks the wealth of options of a classic tourist destination. However, it's tuned to the frequencies of the city's major industries and the visitors they attract from the worlds of business, design and fashion, so a handful of hotels do offer some chic and original choices. The Bulgari (see p022), for example, occupies a modernist block within the gardens of an old monastery, and the Armani Hotel (see p030) is a realisation of the fashion designer's aesthetic inside a rationalist 1937 building. Setting the standard for boutique hotels in this style-conscious city are Palazzo Segreti (opposite); the soft-brutalist Straf (Via San Raffaele 3, T 02 805 081), designed by Vincenzo De Cotiis (see p058); nearby The Gray (see p020); and Magna Pars Suites (see p018) in Zona Tortona. Foresteria Monforte (see p023), meanwhile, is a beautifully appointed guesthouse.

If your taste is more traditional, the Four Seasons (see p019) has rooms within a 15th-century convent, and, just outside the city, the restored Hotel Villa San Carlo Borromeo (Piazza Borromeo 20, Senago, T 02 9950 0722) has long hosted artists and writers, among them Leonardo da Vinci and Stendhal. There are further projects on the immediate horizon. The Mandarin Oriental (Via Monte di Pietà) is redeveloping three graceful 19th-century buildings close to the Quadrilatero della Moda for mid-2015, and a W (Via Brera 19, T 02 63 361) will open its doors in 2016 in the hip Brera district. *For full addresses and room rates, see Resources.*

Palazzo Segreti

On a quiet street near the 15th-century Castello Sforzesco, Palazzo Segreti lives up to its name as something of a hidden spot. Set in a late 19th-century building, the masculine interiors were conceived by owners Roberta and Francesco Tibaldi, and architects Brizzi+Riefenstahl. Exposed brick and concrete are juxtaposed with dark wooden floors and contemporary furnishings in the lobby as well as in the 18 distinct rooms, each of which exudes its own sense of intimacy. The three suites (Room 8, above) benefit from large baths in the bedrooms. Breakfast consists of a fine range of regional produce, a pleasant change from the usual sugary brioche. In the evening, charcuterie, local cheeses and Italian wines are served in the lounge. *Via San Tomaso 8, T 02 4952 9250, www.palazzosegreti.com*

Magna Pars Suites

Situated in the heart of Tortona – Milan's fashion and design hub, and the focus of events during Salone – this supremely stylish hotel, formerly a perfume factory, was refurbished and extended for 2015. The industrial premises have been given a modern eco-friendly makeover and a striking Pompidou-esque glass-and-steel facade. Named after the olfactory notes of flowers and grasses, each of the 39 suites, including Neroli, Jasmine and Abete Bianco (above), have an all-white, pared-down decor with furnishings from Poltrona Frau and Flos. The garden at the centre of the property adds a revitalising aspect, as does the cocktail lounge. Restaurant Da Noi In (T 02 837 8111) champions seasonality and has a strong Italian wine list.
Via Forcella 6, T 02 833 8371, www.magnapars-suitesmilano.com

Four Seasons

The flawless Four Seasons attracts guests enamoured by its proximity to the city's shopping district and the unique setting. The structure incorporates a 17th-century palazzo encircling a secluded courtyard, where it adjoins a converted 15th-century convent. The 118 accommodations here are spread throughout and some look on to the inner courtyard (above); the best are the Cloister Suites, three-storey spaces displaying the remains of original frescoes, and the cosy Renaissance Suite. The work of Filippo Peroni, a set designer for La Scala in the 1800s, can be viewed in the refined Il Foyer lounge/bar and Camino room. In winter, the Four Seasons creates an extravagant Chocolate Room, lined with an array of cocoa-inspired delights. *Via Gesù 6-8, T 02 77 088, www.fourseasons.com/milan*

The Gray
This luxurious hotel by architect Guido Ciompi is a superbly located hideaway next to department store La Rinascente (Piazza del Duomo). The design is sleek but also refreshingly tongue-in-cheek, incorporating such flourishes as a fuchsia-coloured silk swing-seat to greet you in the lobby and suspended four-poster beds in the City Deluxe rooms. In fact, there's welcome variation in the layout of all 21 rooms, which have fantastic bathrooms, some with jacuzzis, others with tubs in the bedroom; we like the Junior Suite 203 (right). For an aperitivo, head to the rooftop Aria Terrace, then enjoy dinner above the Piazza del Duomo at Giacomo Arengario (T 02 7209 3814) on top of the nearby Museo del Novecento (see p078). *Via San Raffaele 6, T 02 720 8951, www.hotelthegray.com*

Bulgari Hotel

The luxury accessory brand's first hotel was created in 2004 by Antonio Citterio and renovated for its 10th anniversary. The 58 rooms are dominated by oak, bronze and black marble, and most have views of the 4,000 sq m gardens that were first tended by monks 300 years ago, providing a serene escape from the buzz of Quadrilatero della Moda. The spa was also updated with the addition of an external jacuzzi and couples' treatment room to the already exceptional facilities, which include a gold mosaic pool and a Turkish bath set in an emerald-glass cube. All rooms feature Citterio's total design; we recommend a Superior Suite or the penthouse Bulgari Suite (terrace, above). In summer, the patio bar is a real hotspot.
Via Privata Fratelli Gabba 7b,
T 02 805 8051, www.bulgarihotels.com

Foresteria Monforte

This charming, affordable *foresteria* (guest house) is a little gem, in a central, largely residential area of the city, five minutes' walk to Piazza San Babila. The amenities are geared towards the self-sufficient traveller (there is no reception or room service) but breakfast is brought to you personally and guests have access to a communal kitchen. There are three airy rooms – two standard, including Centrale (above), and one suite – all looking on to a square, with interiors that combine contemporary and antique furnishings. Owners Giovanni Zonca and Gianni Aporti converted a first-floor apartment above their pharmacy to create the hotel, and its relaxed, affable feel is a real draw. It fills up fast, so reserve well in advance. *Piazza del Tricolore 2, T 02 370 272, www.foresteriamonforte.it*

24 HOURS
SEE THE BEST OF THE CITY IN JUST ONE DAY

Make the city's unparalleled design culture the focus of your day. Fuel up with breakfast at the 1824 Pasticceria Marchesi (Via Santa Maria alla Porta 11a, T 02 862 770), then pay a visit to the Triennale (opposite). You could make an appointment to visit Claudio Loria's contemporary showroom Leclettico (Via San Gregorio 39, T 02 6707 9142) before heading to arts complex La Fabbrica del Vapore (see p026). Spend a few hours in a former workshop or villa of one of Milan's design luminaries, at Studio Museo Achille Castiglioni (see p070), Fondazione Piero Portaluppi (Via Morozzo della Rocca 5, T 02 3652 1591), Vico Magistretti (see p062) or Villa Borsani (Via San Michele 5, Varedo, T 036 258 0304, by appointment). And for an insight into the wealth and taste of the early industrialists, peruse the boudoirs and manicured garden of Villa Necchi (see p028).

Now it's time for that most Milanese part of the day, aperitivo. Via Solferino and its environs offer up manifold enticing bars – Dry (see p031) serves an invigorating French 75 and the best pizza in town. For dinner, head to Turbigo (see p040) or Al Pont de Ferr (Ripa di Porta Ticinese 55, T 02 8940 6277), two of Navigli's more innovative kitchens. A canalside *passeggiata* will afford some of the city's more romantic views, after which you might have room for a cocktail at Elita Bar (Via Corsico 5, T 02 9443 2144) or ice cream at Gelateria della Musica (Via Pestalozzi 4, T 02 3823 5911). *For full addresses, see Resources.*

10.30 Triennale di Milano

Reminiscent of classical architecture with its tall slim arches, Giovanni Muzio's 1933 rationalist building, constructed to host Italy's early expos, became the country's first design museum in 2007. Its extensive collection ranges from the pure functional beauty of Sottsass' typewriters for Olivetti to Gio Ponti's rule-breaking prototypes, displayed in shows such as 'Italian Design Beyond the Crisis', which examines the galvanising effect of austerity on creativity in the 1930s, 1970s and noughties. There are also exhibitions of contemporary art. The sculpture garden features Gaetano Pesce's 'UP5' chair in bronze and Giorgio de Chirico's *Bagni Misteriosi* fountain, the café is furnished with emblematic chairs, and the roof terrace is a fine spot for lunch. *Viale Alemagna 6, T 02 724 341, www.triennale.it*

14.00 La Fabbrica del Vapore
Several of Milan's more interesting
architectural projects have involved
the refurbishment of historic buildings,
many of which date back to the industrial
revolution. One example is La Fabbrica
del Vapore (The Steam Factory), north
of Sempione. Originally the workshop
of the Carminati Toselli company, which
manufactured tramway cars, the entire
complex covers some 30,000 sq m. The
buildings were restored gradually in
phases, with the large shed (right), known
as the Cattedrale (Cathedral) because
of its aisle-like bays, among the last to
be transformed. Today, the site is run
by the city council and used for cultural
events, including visual arts exhibitions
(CARNEM photo project, right) and fashion
shows. Many of the initiatives are aimed
specifically at students. Closed Sundays.
Via Procaccini 4, T 02 996 5885,
www.fabbricadelvapore.org

16.30 Villa Necchi Campiglio

Immortalised in Luca Guadagnino's 2009 film *I Am Love*, this rationalist villa offers a rare glimpse into the private world of Milan's great industrialists. The owners were sisters Gigina and Nedda Necchi, and Gigina's husband, Angelo Campiglio. Manufacturers of cast iron and enamel sewing machines from the 1920s to the 1960s, the family was renowned for its chic parties. The villa was designed by Milanese architect Piero Portaluppi and constructed between 1932 and 1935; it was converted into a museum in 2008. The interiors are a sumptuous combination of walnut, marble and antiques, and Claudia Gian Ferrari's collection of early 20th-century art, which is displayed throughout the house. Open Wednesday to Sunday, 10am to 6pm. *Via Mozart 14, T 02 7634 0121, www.casemuseomilano.it*

18.30 Armani Spa

Located on the eighth floor of the Armani Hotel, within the glass 'hat' perched on Enrico A Griffini's rationalist building, this sleek 1,000 sq m spa has an incredible panorama. The gym, six treatment cabins, couples' room and infinity pool all have views that drink in Milan, so you can work out or simply float about while studying the architectural intricacies of the Duomo (see p014). Muted tones, green river stone, tatami mats and olive leather on the walls help keep the surroundings unmistakably Armani. Spa treatments are grouped into three menus, each focusing on a different outcome – relaxation, rejuvenation or detoxification – and you book a time slot, rather than a particular therapy. Open daily from 9am to 9pm. *Armani Hotel, Via Manzoni 31, T 02 8883 8888, www.armanihotels.com*

SAZERAC
HANKY PANKY
CORPSE REVIVER #2
RAMOS GIN FIZZ
MARTINEZ

22.00 Dry

The owners of neighbouring Pisacco (T 02 9176 5472) have struck gold again here. Chef Andrea Berton, who earned Michelin stars at Trussardi alla Scala (T 02 8068 8201) and Ristorante Berton (T 02 6707 5801), dreamt up this superior pizza-and-cocktails concept. Designed by Vudafieri Saverino Partners, the industrial-chic space features brass, mirrors and vintage school furniture. Niek Van der Heijden's 'Living Forum' is another seating option: zinc tubing joins six mismatched chairs in a circle, a set-up designed to encourage conversation. The Peep-Hole Gallery (see p069) curates the video art. Sample the focaccia with datterino tomatoes and stracciatella (fresh cream cheese), and a negroni mixed with barrel-aged campari. *Via Solferino 33, T 02 6379 3414, www.drymilano.it*

URBAN LIFE
CAFÉS, RESTAURANTS, BARS AND NIGHTCLUBS

This is a city on the up, and excellent options abound. There is a multitude of experimental bars, such as Dry (see p031) and Carlo e Camilla (see p034), in which to take your aperitivo, or try one of the born-again traditional venues like the 1896 dance hall La Balera dell'Ortica (Via Amadeo 78, T 02 7012 8680) and elegantly renovated Drogheria Parini (see p050). In a fertile restaurant scene, the innovative Turbigo (see p040) and A Casa Eatery (see p044) are blazing a trail and setting the tone for the next generation.

Some things never change – this is, after all, Italy. Good coffee is easy to find, although avoid ordering a cappuccino after midday if you don't want to be sneered at (it's strictly macchiato and caffè post-noon). Meanwhile, pizza and focaccia are served in modern settings these days, at Breri (Via Pontaccio 5, T 02 3673 7385) and Princi (Piazza XXV Aprile 5, T 02 2906 0832). Like a stylish *nonna*, many fashion stores want to feed you as well, as at Trussardi alla Scala (see p031), Emporio Armani Caffè (Via Croce Rossa 2, T 02 6231 2680) and 10 Corso Como (Corso Como 10, T 02 2901 3581).

For that quintessential Milan experience, drop in to Pasticceria Taveggia (Via Visconti di Modrone 2, T 02 7628 0856) for a pick-me-up, eat at Trattoria del Nuovo Macello (see p039) or Il Salumaio di Montenapoleone (see p046), and sip a negroni among the mosaics at Il Camparino (Galleria Vittorio Emanuele II, T 02 8646 4435). *For full addresses, see Resources.*

Larte

Inspired by the Altagamma Foundation luxury trade group, Larte is the fruit of a collaboration between several prestigious Italian brands, including Alessi, Caffarel, Bellavista, San Pellegrino and Artemide. The multi-faceted space encompasses a retail gallery of art and design alongside a *cioccolateria*, and also has a theatre and exhibition area. Bespoke fixtures and fittings by the likes of Achille Castiglioni and Carlo Mollino establish the creative tone, enhanced by artworks by Arnaldo Pomodoro and Alberto Burri, which is further reinforced by the restaurant's fine modern Italian cuisine. Order the strips of beef with porcini and egg salsa, or the thin tagliatelle with lemon, soft cheese, sea asparagus and shrimp.
Via Manzoni 5, T 02 8909 6950,
www.lartemilano.com

Carlo e Camilla
Polished antique chandeliers, Cappellini
chairs, Richard Ginori tableware and a
majolica-tiled bar contrast with the brick
and cement shell of this former sawmill.
Reservations on the two communal tables
in designer Tanja Solci and TV chef Carlo
Cracco's restaurant can be hard to secure,
but fortunately the bar serves imaginative
cocktails with no waiting required.
Via Giuseppe Meda 24, T 02 837 3963

Ceresio 7

Atop the 1930s Enel Building, Ceresio 7 was launched in 2013 by Dsquared2's Dean and Dan Caten, with help from architects Storage. Open until 1am, it attracts a beautifully turned-out crowd in summer to two outdoor pools flanked by cabanas and terraces with wraparound views, and year-round to the restaurant and bar, where Dimore Studio's interiors pay homage to the building's rationalist heritage. Among the mix of vintage and contemporary are decorative elements such as a Gio Ponti tea set. Chef Elio Sironi adds a twist to traditional Italian dishes, many cooked on the grill or in the wood oven. Try the lobster linguine with chilli flakes and courgette, followed by Vignola cherries in spiced red wine and chocolate.
Via Ceresio 7, T 02 3103 9221,
www.ceresio7.com

Un Posto a Milano

A renovated late 17th-century communal farmhouse, typical of northern Italy, Cascina Cuccagna is at odds with the surrounding apartment blocks of Porta Romana. Taken over by a coalition of community enterprises on a mission to revitalise these historic buildings, the 4,000 sq m site now features a bicycle repair shop (Saturdays only), a deli, a hostel and the restaurant Un Posto a Milano. The interior is composed of raw wood furniture and clean, modern details, and the garden is a supreme place to relax with a chilled glass of wine. Locally sourced food includes hearty fare like vegetable pie and focaccia with aged salami. On Tuesdays (3pm to 9.30pm) there's a farmers' market and aperitivo tasting in the courtyard.
Via Cuccagna 2, T 02 545 7785,
www.unpostoamilano.it

Trattoria del Nuovo Macello

Milan's historic food markets are still very much in operation in this residential area in the east of the city, and Trattoria del Nuovo Macello has fed and watered local workers since 1957. It remains an isolated outpost, retaining its antique interior and utilising super-fresh produce. The family owners revitalised the place in the late 1990s, introducing inventive versions of Lombardy's traditional cuisine, such as the spaghetti with ricotta, lemon, red onion and anchovies. Make a booking and take a taxi to this hidden gem. Nearby, contemporary sister restaurant, Cucina dei Frigoriferi (T 02 739 8245), has opened within the grounds of the industrial-space-turned-cultural-centre Frigoriferi Milanesi, and specialises in fish dishes.
Via Cesare Lombroso 20, T 02 5990 2122, www.trattoriadelnuovomacello.it

Turbigo

In a small hotel in Navigli, Turbigo is a modern take on the canalside vernacular. The rustic feel is offset by neon lettering, a Patrizia Cantarella-curated wall of art, and Ingo Maurer lights above a stone bench and wood and plastic furnishings. Chef Raffaele Lenzi serves creative Italian cuisine, from breakfast to dinner. *Alzaia Naviglio Grande 8, T 02 8940 0407, www.turbigomilano.it*

Fioraio Bianchi Caffè

While exploring Brera, this little gem is a delightful place to have lunch. Raimondo Bianchi's renowned florist of 48 years was renovated by the Milan-based Sicilian Ivan Marino, and flowers still fill the space. The architect stripped off a century of cement to reveal the original walls and floor, and turned a stone basin (once used to wash flowers) into a small fountain in the dining area. The bar was constructed from a 300-year-old pulpit, and the restored chairs date to 1900. The food is just as carefully composed, ranging from roasted bream with stewed aubergine to crème brûlée infused with lavender and Sicilian *cassata* (ricotta cake), and a fantastic selection of regional wines. Even a quick macchiato at this lovely venue restores the spirit. *Via Montebello 7, T 02 2901 4390, www.fioraiobianchicaffe.it*

A Casa Eatery

At first glance, A Casa Eatery appears not to be a restaurant at all but a sprawling, well-appointed apartment. Architect Giovanna Carboni selected all the vintage furniture, including the saddle racks, the baskets once used to collect local arborio rice, the child-size dining table and tiny chairs, and the chest of drawers with wire fronts for pasta storage. Wooden shelves are lined with jams and dried goods for sale, as well as bottles of *rosolio*, a rose-petal liqueur from Puglia. Straightforward cooking focuses on the powerful flavours of southern Italy, such as the tender octopus, which is soaked in salt water and pounded soft, Mediterranean-style, then served in red wine. The desserts, prepared by pastry chef Andrea Regonati, are exquisite, especially the signature *pasticciotto* (custard tarts) from Salento.
Via Conca del Naviglio 37, T 02 3674 3350, www.acasaeatery.it

Il Salumaio di Montenapoleone
A renowned delicatessen since 1957, Il Salumaio opened this restaurant and a café in the stables of the Palazzo Bagatti Valsecchi villa museum in 2011. The cuisine is simple and classic: fresh pasta, veal cutlet in breadcrumbs, fine cheeses and meats. In summer, reserve a table in the courtyard under the lemon tree. *Via Santo Spirito 10/Via Gesù 5, T 02 7600 1123, www.ilsalumaiodimontenapoleone.it*

28 Posti

As the name suggests, this venue, visible from the street through glass-front arches, has 28 seats. Each one, plus all the tables, doors and cabinets, has been crafted by inmates from the city's Bollate prison to designs by Francesco Faccin and made using reclaimed materials, as are Alvaro Catalán de Ocón's 'PET' lamps. The photos on the breeze-block walls are by Filippo Romano. Energetic chef Marco Ambrosino turns his hand to everything from bread to dessert, using organic, local ingredients where possible to create Mediterranean dishes such as potato ravioli with goat's cheese, red shrimp, oranges and walnuts, and a super weekend brunch. On the same street are two great cocktail bars: Ugo (T 02 339 123 4203) and Elita (see p024). *Via Corsico 1, T 02 839 2377, www.28posti.org*

Pavè

Three friends – Giovanni Giberti, Luca Scanni and Diego Bamberghi – are behind Pavè, which opened in 2012 in the most multicultural area of Milan, close to Corso Buenos Aires. The café/deli has fast gained a reputation for its *pasticcini* and bread, which are prepared on the premises. Made with stoneground flour, the loaves are taken out of the oven every day at 3pm, in time for those returning home from work.

For breakfast, sample the brioche with Madagascan vanilla cream, or *sbrisolona*, a traditional Lombardy cake. At weekends, the *millefoglie espressa*, a puff-pastry cake filled with cream, is made to order in eight minutes. Pavè's eclectic interior is as joyous as the food, and features a cheerful combination of reclaimed furnishings.
Via Casati 27, T 02 9439 2259,
www.pavemilano.com

Drogheria Parini
Gio Pagani presented Parini with a
makeover for its centenary by stripping
the storeroom ceiling to reveal the brick
arches that once housed a crypt. They
now frame a restaurant/bar, decorated
with mirrors and marble, in which chef
Marco Parizzi creates refined versions
of classics such as osso buco. The food
emporium, dating from 1915, remains.
Via Borgospesso 1, T 02 3668 3500

Al Fresco

The brainchild of landscape architect Emanuele Bortolotti and wine-bar owner Ferdinando Ferdinandi, Al Fresco, in buzzy Tortona, has a contemporary interior with a verdant, airy greenhouse-cum-artist's-studio ambience. But the name of the restaurant reveals the real star here: the lovingly tended green refuge just visible from the street through the vast windows of this former warehouse. Visit on a warm day for a table among the cherry trees, honeysuckle, wisteria and herbs. Chef Kokichi Takahashi uses flavours inspired by the garden. Order the carnaroli risotto with sweet pepper, paprika, burrata cheese and liquorice powder, and make room for the much-loved bread from Matera that accompanies every meal.

Via Savona 50, T 02 4953 3630,
www.alfrescomilano.it

Erba Brusca

Located in an idyllic spot south of the city centre, this bright, breezy restaurant was designed by the Milan-based Rgastudio, which channelled the spirit of the venue's canalside location in creating the interior. The restaurant's founder, Alice Delcourt, was born in France and raised in the US, but has long harboured a passion for Italy and its food. She honed her culinary skills in numerous restaurants before striking out on her own here in 2011. The vegetable garden lends Erba Brusca a bucolic aspect but the ambience is utterly cosmopolitan. The homegrown produce appears in dishes such as tarte tatin with aubergine, tomatoes and stracciatella. If you'd like to cycle along the canal, you can hire your wheels here. Open Wednesday to Sunday.
Alzaia Naviglio Pavese 286, T 02 8738 0711, www.erbabrusca.it

INSIDER'S GUIDE

CAROLINE CORBETTA, CURATOR

Scandurra Studio's Expo Gate (opposite; Via Luca Beltrami), the twin glass pyramids in the heart of the city, have been transformed into a vibrant cultural platform under the stewardship of Caroline Corbetta. 'Milan's remarkable dynasty of designers, architects and artists makes me proud and gives me hope for the future,' she says.

For an overview, she suggests the Renaissance masterpieces in Pinacoteca di Brera (Via Brera 28, T 02 7226 3264); Michelangelo's *Pietà Rondanini* in Castello Sforzesco (Piazza Castello, T 02 8846 3700); Cimitero Monumentale (Piazzale Cimitero Monumentale 1), essentially an open-air museum of 150 years of sculpture; design studio Fondazione Franco Albini (Via Telesio 13, T 02 498 2378); and the contemporary galleries Zero (Viale Premuda 46, T 02 8723 4577) and Giò Marconi (Via Alessandro Tadino 15, T 02 2940 4373).

Corbetta likes to treat herself to breakfast at the poolside café at Villa Necchi Campiglio (see p028). She is a regular at Il Carpaccio (via Lazzaro Palazzi 19, T 02 2940 5982), for its 'authentic, home-style cooking', and curates a mini-gallery in the trattoria's window. She recommends the classic charm of old-school wine bar Cantine Isola (Via Paolo Sarpi 30, T 02 331 5249) and on special occasions she books a table at Ristorante Cracco (Via Victor Hugo 4, T 02 876 774), Berton (see p031) or D'O (Via Magenta 18, Cornaredo, T 02 936 2209): 'These three chefs are creating a culinary revolution.' *For full addresses, see Resources.*

ART AND DESIGN
GALLERIES, STUDIOS AND PUBLIC SPACES

Salone del Mobile casts the spotlight on Milan, but the city dazzles all year round thanks to a surfeit of locally based talent that helps maintain the potency of the 'Made in Italy' label. The nexus of the furniture industry is Brianza, where the great masters developed their ideas in close collaboration with highly skilled artisans and manufacturers, a process beautifully illustrated in Milan's studio museums (see p024). The work of today's generation is on display in galleries like De Cotiis (see p058) and Dimore (see p066).

Complementing Salone, art fair Miart has taken off, stimulated by the vitality of spaces such as Kaufmann Repetto (see p059), Lia Rumma (see p069) and Fluxia (Via Ventura 6, T 02 2171 1913), set in an old scooter factory in Lambrate, a vibrant creative hub that encapsulates the scene. In fact, the private sphere has long been progressive, even as the council continues to focus on Leonardo da Vinci – pay homage at Pinacoteca Ambrosiana (Piazza Pio XI, T 02 8069 2215). And it is commercial largesse that is giving the city the contemporary institutions it deserves. Pirelli's HangarBicocca (see p060) has been joined by Gallerie d'Italia (Piazza della Scala 6, T 800 167 619), a neoclassical palazzo filled with Banco Sanpaolo's collection of 19th- and 20th-century work. Opening for Expo is OMA's conversion of a century-old distillery, complete with quirky tower, to house the Museo della Fondazione Prada (Largo Isarco). *For full addresses, see Resources.*

Chiesa Rossa

US artist Dan Flavin completed the plans for this, his untitled final work, just days before his death in 1996. The installation of blue, green, red and gold neon within the church of Santa Maria Annunciata in Chiesa Rossa was facilitated with the help of New York's Dia Art Foundation and the Fondazione Prada (opposite), which commissioned the piece. The church itself is a 1932 creation by the prolific Giovanni Muzio (see p025), designed in the classical style of purified grandeur that had found favour during the fascist era. Flavin always rejected spiritual readings of his abstract compositions, but the transcendental overtones of this sublimely serene work in its remarkable ecclesiastical setting seem to reflect a more mystical vision at the end of his life. It is best viewed at dusk. *Via Neera 24, www.smacr.com*

Galleria De Cotiis

You may well first encounter architect and designer Vincenzo De Cotiis' reconstructed, sculptural aesthetic in the Straf Hotel (see p016) or Antonia (see p085). The organic, disassembled forms and outlines of his Progetto Domestico label take inspiration from art deco, the 1980s, fin-de-siècle Vienna, futurists such as Bruno Munari and modern artists like Nanda Vigo and Alessandro Mendini. De Cotiis' Reflective Subjects range is as tactile as it is visual, contrasting gleaming metal with salvaged materials and rough textures, recycled wood, fibreglass, resin and leather. Pieces such as the 'DC1401B' onyx table with brass legs and the 'DC1406B' silver-plated LED chandelier (both above) are offset by the minimalism of his showroom.
Via Carlo de Cristoforis 14, T 02 8728 7757, www.decotiis.it

Kaufmann Repetto

In 2010, the eclectic gallery run by sisters Francesca Kaufmann and Chiara Repetto relocated to a more spacious concrete-floored space beside Parco Sempione designed by Frank Boehm. It now hosts a project room dedicated to experimental work by young artists, with everything from multimedia and performance art to photography and painting, plus outdoor sculptures displayed in the courtyard. It is admired for exhibiting fresh, compelling pieces by artists including Eva Rothschild, Pae White, Adrian Paci and Thea Djordjadze ('Oxymoron Grey', above), as well as for championing new talent. Nearby, the chic Bottega del Vino (T 02 3493 6128) and Cantine Isola (see p054) are both superior options for a post-show glass of wine. *Via di Porta Tenaglia 7, T 02 7209 4331, www.kaufmannrepetto.com*

HangarBicocca

The north-eastern industrial district of Bicocca was occupied by the vast Pirelli complex until the mid-1980s, when the company began one of Europe's most ambitious regeneration projects. The area now accommodates multinationals, a university, student dorms and, since 2004, HangarBicocca, a contemporary art museum that is based in and around a former engine-coil factory. It's home to large-scale installations that include *La Sequenza* (pictured) by Fausto Melotti, inspired by ancient Greek architecture, Piero della Francesca and Bach; Anselm Kiefer's haunting *The Seven Heavenly Palaces*; and provocative temporary exhibits by international artists. Open Thursday to Sunday, 11am to midnight. *Via Chiese 2, T 02 6611 1573, www.hangarbicocca.org*

Fondazione Vico Magistretti

Milanese architect and designer Vico Magistretti was a major figure of 20th-century Italian design. In the 1940s and 1950s, he contributed to plans for the experimental neighbourhood QT8 on the edge of the city, as well as an estate for Pirelli workers. In product design, he focused on functional furniture that could be mass-produced, creating classics such as the 'Carimate' chair for Cassina.

The studio where he worked for 60 years is open to visitors, and offers two design excursions: one is a tour of 14 of his most important buildings in Milan; the other comprises visits to companies affiliated with the designer. Open Tuesdays (10am to 6pm), Thursdays (2pm to 8pm) and on Saturdays by appointment (2pm to 6pm). *Via Conservatorio 20, T 02 7600 2964, www.vicomagistretti.it*

Oeuffice

Canadian designers Jakub Zak and Nicolas Bellavance-Lecompte first met in Milan in 2011 and began creating pieces that resemble monuments. The first collection, Totems for Living, featured towering, repetitive structures intended to be used as display units; this was followed up with Ziggurats – stacked piles of boxes in art deco styles that perform a similar shrine-like function. Kapital, the designers' 2014 series, is a pared-down vision of classical architecture, with stone tables and stools in handcarved Italian marble referencing the columns of antiquity. 'Tuskan' (above), €4,500, amalgamates an abacus of *nero assoluto* granite with a shaft of travertine and a base of *giallo reale* marble. Pieces are available to buy at the apartment-style gallery Le Stanze di Dimore (see p066). *www.oeuffice.com*

L.O.V.E.

Artist Maurizio Cattelan is perhaps Milan's most mischievous son. In 2010, he unveiled a sculpture of a 4m-tall hand, beautifully carved in classical Carrara marble, with only the middle finger remaining. Cattelan has called it a commentary on the fascist salute and a criticism of totalitarianism, and it is placed right in front of the stock exchange in the 1932 Palazzo Mezzanotte. Just as Wall Street's charging bull is a symbol of the optimism of its era, the sculpture has come to embody negativity towards the establishment, but it is not clear whether the gesture is directed at the bankers or if it symbolises the industry's wider message to the world. Its official title, *L.O.V.E.*, is an acronym in Italian for freedom, hate, revenge, eternity – locals simply refer to it as *Il Dito* (The Finger). *Piazza Affari*

Galleria Post Design

This gallery exhibits key creations from the riotous Memphis group, which defined postmodern design through its furniture, lighting, glassware and jewellery. Ettore Sottsass, whose graphic, multicoloured, iconic 'Carlton' room divider arguably best embodies the Memphis spirit, formed the movement in Milan in 1981 with Nathalie du Pasquier and Matteo Thun, using cheap materials, vivid tones and irrationality to reject Bauhaus functionalism. The gallery also hosts contemporary designers such as Giacomo Moor, who depicts cityscapes in wood (walnut 'Tecla' wardrobe and 'Dedalus' bookcase, above). Many of the Memphis pieces – from the 'Murmansk' fruit bowl by Sottsass to Marco Zanini's 'Colorado' teapot – are perfectly portable. *Via della Moscova 27, T 02 655 4731, www.memphis-milano.it*

Le Stanze Di Dimore
Part workshop, part gallery, Dimore is set
in a former apartment of an 18th-century
palazzo, and the warren of rooms here
maintains a domestic intimacy. Furniture
and interior design by owners Britt Moran
and Emiliano Salci, and others (see p063),
as well as the vintage pieces for which it is
known, are arranged in inviting tableaux.
Via Solferino 11, T 02 3653 7088,
www.dimorestudio.eu

Spazio Rossana Orlandi

Housed in a former tie factory and set around a vine-filled garden courtyard, this two-storey emporium displays creative contemporary and vintage interior design and also hosts one of the most important and reliably amusing presentations during Salone del Mobile. Rossana Orlandi has helped launch the careers of such globally recognised names as Jaime Hayon, Nacho Carbonell and Piet Hein Eek, and she continues to exhibit some of the most consistently original pieces year-round. Amid the neat rows of old tie drawers you might find Maarten Baas' lumpy 'Clay' chairs, Gaetano Pesce's moulded foam foot, colour-diffracting lights by Dennis Parren or Toronto studio UUfie's Corian 'Peacock' chair (above). *Via Matteo Bandello 14-16, T 02 467 4471, www.rossanaorlandi.com*

Galleria Lia Rumma

Near Cimiterio Monumentale (see p054), unassuming Via Stilicone has morphed into a small arts district as old workshops are converted into studios. The catalyst was Fonderia Battaglia (T 02 341 071), a foundry that for more than a century has cast bronze statues for sculptors of the calibre of Arnaldo Pomodoro. In the same building, Peep-Hole (T 02 8706 7410) focuses on experimental video and installations. Down the street, Galleria Lia Rumma hosts thought-provoking work by artists such as Vanessa Beecroft, Enrico Castellan, Anselm Kiefer and Alberto Burri. Converted by CLS architects, the stark white three-storey box is softened by a first-floor terrace and a rooftop event space. Open Tuesday to Saturday.
Via Stilicone 19, T 02 2900 0101,
www.liarumma.it

Studio Museo Achille Castiglioni
This museum is situated in the Milan studio
where Achille Castiglioni worked for 40
years until his death in 2002. It was opened
to the public in 2006, and provides a
unique insight into the outstanding career
and rich legacy of one of Italy's most
highly respected design talents, with the
intact studio granting a rare opportunity
to view the process behind Castiglioni's
art. Marvel at the collection of everyday
objects – his 'tools of design instruction',
some of which inspired his most celebrated
projects – and the huge number of photos,
sketches, prototypes and models that he
produced. The museum is open 10am to
1pm weekdays and, in April during Salone
del Mobile, at weekends too. Phone for
an appointment to join the hourly tours.
Piazza Castello 27, T 02 805 3606,
www.achillecastiglioni.it

ARCHITOUR
A GUIDE TO MILAN'S ICONIC BUILDINGS

It should be said that Milan has never been the first port of call for architecture fans. Apart from the Duomo (see p014), which took 424 years to complete and runs the gamut of styles from Gothic to Renaissance, and its idiosyncratic neighbour, Torre Velasca (see p011), it has otherwise been characterised by blocks of anonymous towers that replaced the bombsites in the postwar boom years.

Yet today a new cosmopolitanism and dynamism is pervading the city's famously smoggy air, which is itself being redressed in a slew of headline-grabbing projects championing environmental sustainability. From Porta Nuova (opposite) to CityLife (see p009), parks and museums, which have traditionally been neglected in Milan, figure prominently. And then there's Expo, where many of the pavilions by architects including Foster + Partners, Italo Rota, Arthur Casas and Daniel Libeskind will be dismantled to leave a vast green lung beside the eco-conscious Fiera Milano (see p074).

Individual gems from all eras dot the city, of course. Seek out the Palazzo dell'Arengario (see p078), a benchmark of rationalist architecture; Tadao Ando's hauntingly ethereal Teatro Armani (Via Bergognone 59), a factory conversion from 2000; the noughties brutalism of Università Bocconi (see p076); and curiosities like the concrete igloos of Villaggio dei Giornalisti (Via Lepanto). Milan's architectural hero, though, will always be Gio Ponti (see p075). *For full addresses, see Resources.*

Bosco Verticale

Another eye-catching Porta Nuova project, Bosco Verticale is a pair of residential towers, made unorthodox by virtue of the 11,000 plants, 5,000 shrubs and 900 trees that soften its facade. Designed by Boeri Studio and built on a vacant lot, the blocks rise to 112m and 80m, and are a prototype for an environmental solution to Milan's density and air pollution problems. This 'Vertical Forest' topped out in 2014, and, added together, its greenery represents the equivalent of a hectare of foliage. The complexities of growing large trees on the balconies that adorn the 27 storeys necessitated a raft of engineering feats, as well as the implementation of a recycled grey-water irrigation system. Integrated photovoltaic panels provide energy.
Via Gaetano de Castillia/Via Federico Confalonieri

Fiera Milano

Next to the Expo site, a 25-minute metro ride from the city centre, Massimiliano and Doriana Fuksas' 2005 trade-fair complex was part of a massive regeneration project. Built on the grounds of an old oil refinery in just 24 months at a cost of €750m, the exhibition area alone covers 345,000 sq m. The central element is a ribbon-like glass-and-steel canopy that stretches for 1.3km, enveloping the buildings along its path. It ends in a crater-like vortex at either side. Several innovative solutions were devised to help keep the development as green as possible. Perhaps the most interesting is the photocatalytic paint that was used to treat the pavilions: the 100,000 sq m of coated surfaces is said to neutralise the air pollution produced by 15,000 cars. *Strada Statale del Sempione 28, T 02 49 971, www.fieramilano.it*

Chiesa di San Francesco al Fopponino

The Pirelli Tower (see p013) is Gio Ponti's best-known building in Milan, where he worked all his life, but his contribution to the city includes other notable structures: his twin offices at Via Moscova 3/Largo Donegani 2, built in 1936 and 1951 for the Montecatini company, and two arresting churches. The Chiesa di San Francesco, a collaboration with Antonio Fornaroli and Alberto Rosselli, was completed in 1964.

The facade is clad in diamond-shaped tiles and set back from the street, with the east and west wings recessed further, providing a screen for the courtyards behind. The configuration of the tiles and hexagonal windows are typical Ponti motifs; those to either side of the nave are open, framing the sky. Ponti's Chiesa dell'Ospedale San Carlo, finished in 1967, is on Via Papa Pio. *Via Giovio 41, www.fopponino.it*

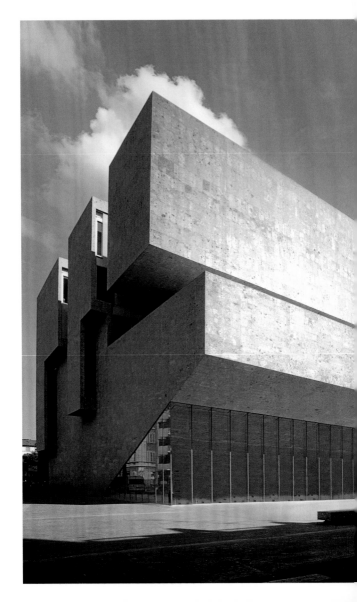

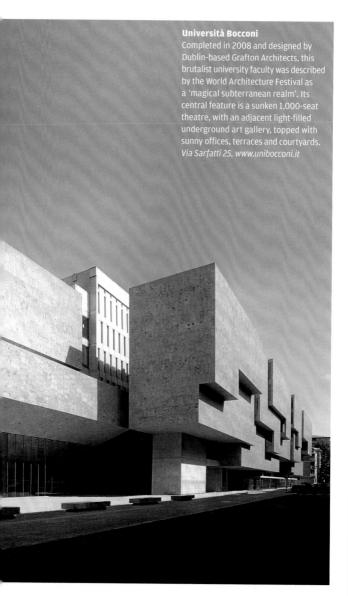

Università Bocconi
Completed in 2008 and designed by Dublin-based Grafton Architects, this brutalist university faculty was described by the World Architecture Festival as a 'magical subterranean realm'. Its central feature is a sunken 1,000-seat theatre, with an adjacent light-filled underground art gallery, topped with sunny offices, terraces and courtyards. *Via Sarfatti 25, www.unibocconi.it*

Museo del Novecento

The city's contemporary art collection had been sitting in storage for 12 years until it was given a new home in 2010 with the highly anticipated conversion of Palazzo dell'Arengario, a fascist-era relic adorned with lovely bas reliefs by Arturo Martini that was only finished in 1956. Architects Italo Rota and Fabio Fornasari conceived a discreet, light-filled structure incorporating a spiralling indoor ramp that connects the underground level to a terrace overlooking Piazza del Duomo. An external staircase and covered walkway connects adjacent Palazzo Reale to the stylish rooftop bar and restaurant Giacomo Arengario (see p020). The permanent collection is superb, with particularly strong sections dedicated to the futurists, spatialism and Arte Povera. *Via Marconi 1, T 02 8844 4061, www.museodelnovecento.org*

SHOPS
THE BEST RETAIL THERAPY AND WHAT TO BUY

One of Milan's top attractions is its shopping, notably around the Quadrilatero of Via Manzoni, Via Montenapoleone, Via della Spiga and Via Sant'Andrea. The luxury brands are all here, from Missoni (see p090) to Giorgio Armani (Via Montenapoleone 2, T 02 7600 3234), plus local favourites like Aspesi (see p088) and women's boutique No 30 (Via della Spiga 30, T 02 7631 7377), as well as Tadao Ando's Duvetica store (Via Santo Spirito 22, T 02 7602 2967) and the sleek Herno (Via Sant'Andrea 14, T 02 9443 2789). Nearby, the glorious gilded arcades of Galleria Vittorio Emanuele II have been restored, with the bill footed by Prada (see p093), Feltrinelli and Versace, which opened a flagship here in 2014.

Around Via Durini, you'll find the design heavyweights such as B&B Italia (No 14, T 02 764 441) and Flos (Corso Monforte 15, T 02 798 457), although there are interiors showrooms throughout the city: Azucena (opposite), Fragile (overleaf) and Spotti (Viale Piave 27, T 02 781 953) are all inspiring spaces. Also in this area is Dolce & Gabbana's multi-brand boutique Piave 37 (Viale Piave 37, T 02 2951 1408), which promotes emerging designers. In Zona Tortona, check out Antonio Marras' concept store (Via Cola di Rienzo 8, T 02 8907 5002) and browse for vintage Italian design in the antiques market held on the last Sunday of the month along the Naviglio Grande canal, when the local bars and restaurants open all day. *For full addresses, see Resources.*

Azucena

This snug showroom, opened in 2013, is tucked away off a palazzo courtyard, a suitable setting for the firm established in Milan in 1947 by a quintet of creatives led by architect Luigi Caccia Dominioni. Dimore Studio (see p066) has maintained its historic character, with grey walls and brass detailing adding a sobriety to the refined setting. Contemporary pieces sit alongside classic Azucena designs, and Dominioni's work prevails – as does the man himself, standing guard in a black and white photograph hung above the stairs. The showroom offers visitors a career-spanning survey of his output, from 1953's slender 'LTE5 Imbuto' floor lamp to the svelte 'P17 Sant'Ambrogio' sofa, designed in 1981 (both above).
Via Manzoni 23, T 02 781 926,
www.azucena.it

Fragile
A colourful repudiation of the minimal
design gallery scene, Fragile, with its
seafoam-green walls and puzzle-pattern
tiled floor, is a vibrant two-storey space
designed by Atelier Mendini and styled
by Studiopepe. It sells work by the
rowdier designers of the 20th century,
such as Gino Sarfatti, Franco Albini and
Gio Ponti, as well as vintage jewellery.
Via San Damiano 2, T 02 3656 1161

Pirelli

This is a fitting flagship for the ground-breaking Milanese company, which was founded by engineer Giovanni Battista Pirelli back in 1872. Designed by architect Renato Montagner, the store brings the label's fashion lines together under one roof for the first time, in an edgy 1,500 sq m space. PZero clothing and footwear ranges are displayed in an environment that references Pirelli's better-known automotive activities, with rubber floors and a wall made from the soundproofing material that's used in the tyre-testing factory. One room shows a collection of memorabilia from the archives, including photos, advertising campaigns and artist Bruno Munari's 'Meo Romeo' bendy toy cat, which he designed in 1949.
Corso Venezia 1, T 02 6442 4242, www.pirellipzero.com

Antonia

The 19th-century Palazzo Cagnola once housed the offices of Joseph Radetzky, the Austrian general who defeated the Italian patriots in 1849. For the arrival of Antonia Giacinti's unisex multi-brand 600 sq m fashion emporium, Vincenzo De Cotiis (see p058) stripped back the stone walls and left them partially bare to contrast with his dazzling lighting and polished furnishings; the plush rugs are by Nilufar (see p091). The clothing is from brands such as Lanvin, Balenciaga, Chloé and Fendi, with accessories by the likes of René Caovilla, Christian Louboutin and Bruno Frisoni. It's worth checking out the new names, too, as Giacinti has an eye for talent. She also curated luxury department store Excelsior (T 02 7630 7301).
Via Cusani 5, T 02 8699 8340, www.antonia.it

Kiton

The luxury menswear brand created by Cira Paone reopened its expanded retail space in 2011 in honour of the addition of a womenswear line, and the elegant store now features walnut panelling, black marble details and bronze fixtures. Kiton oversees every detail of its collections, from the quality of the thread used in its fabrics to the tailoring school it operates to produce the top-of-the-line suits, very much in keeping with the grand sartorial tradition of its birthplace in Naples. In a show of force, Kiton recently acquired the 1910 Liberty palazzo that was once the home of fashion designer Gianfranco Ferré, architect Franco Raggi restoring the building and converting it into a corporate showroom and headquarters. Paone's art collection lines the walls, including works by Mimmo Paladino and Lucio Del Pezzo. *Via Gesù 11, T 02 7639 0240, www.kiton.it*

Aspesi

Alberto Aspesi's clothing for men and women has come to define a certain Milanese style – excellent fabrics and tailoring with timeless design. This store by Antonio Citterio and Partners and creative agency Tomato is a draw by itself, due to Aspesi's contemporary art collection, with pieces by the likes of Jannis Kounellis and Mario Merz.
Via Montenapoleone 13, T 02 7602 2478

Missoni

In collaboration with creative director Angela Missoni, designer Patricia Urquiola set about reimagining Missoni's flagship store in the epicentre of the Quadrilatero. Taking the label's distinctive patterns and textures as their inspiration, the duo devised a sophisticated scheme of striped panels, boiserie and coloured display units, suspending the clothes from slender wooden rails. With its hint of retro chic, the interior of contrasting surfaces and colours is an inspired backdrop for the brand, a Milan institution that celebrated its 60th year in 2013. This is Missoni's only stand-alone store in the city, and it carries the full range of fashions and accessories for men, women and children. Note that the entrance is on Via Sant'Andrea.

Via Montenapoleone 8, T 02 7600 3555, www.missoni.it

Nilufar

Launched in 1979 by Nina Yashar, who named the store after her sister, Nilu, Nilufar began as a showcase for seminal 20th-century design and oriental carpets. Today, it is a go-to for devotees of both modernist and contemporary pieces. A Formica-topped desk designed by Gio Ponti for Vembi-Burroughs in the 1950s and a 1957 walnut bed by Franco Albini and Franca Helg for Poggi (both above) were some of the gems we spied on our visit. Nilufar appears at Design Miami/ Basel and also hosts its own exhibitions, which can be wonderfully eclectic, showing works by the likes of Ignazio Gardella, Piero Fornasetti, Gaetano Pesce, Jacques Adnet and Paul Evans. A judicious selection of more recent design is also sold in store. *Via della Spiga 32, T 02 780 193, www.nilufar.com*

Galleria Anna Maria Consadori

Daughter of the Italian painter Silvio Consadori, Anna Maria trained as an architect before opening this showroom selling Italian design from the 1930s onwards. Her taste is impeccable; pieces on sale have included sculptures by Gio Pomodoro and Mario Negri, expressionist ceramics by Lucio Fontana, paintings by Roberto Crippa and chairs by Giulio Minoletti. Consadori's father taught at the neighbouring Accademia di Belle Arti di Brera in the 17th-century Palazzo Brera, also home to the Pinacoteca di Brera (see p054). This is one of Italy's more prominent museums for Renaissance art, and has a collection spanning the 13th to the 20th centuries, including works by Piero della Francesca, Caravaggio and Tintoretto. *Via Brera 2, T 02 7202 1767, www.galleriaconsadori.com*

Prada

This is where it all began. The first Prada store, a leather goods shop, was opened inside Galleria Vittorio Emanuele II in 1913 by Mario Prada, Miuccia's grandfather. It retains many original features, such as the Belgian marble floor and mahogany and brass furniture; a pair of glass vitrines display some of the shop's original goods. There are five other Prada outposts in town: a menswear store on the other side of the arcade (T 02 8721 1450); adjacent showrooms on Via Montenapoleone, stocking menswear (T 02 7602 0273) and women's ready-to-wear (T 02 777 1771); Via della Spiga (T 02 780 465), which sells women's accessories; and Corso Venezia (T 02 7600 1426), which carries shoes and accessories for both men and women. *Galleria Vittorio Emanuele II 63-65, T 02 876 979, www.prada.com*

Villa Meissen

The 300-year-old Meissen porcelain company chose Milan for its European flagship, opening this showroom in 2012 in one of the city's foremost villas. Painstakingly restored, the 16th-century Casa Carcassola-Grandi is replete with architectural features, including a neoclassical facade designed in the early 19th century by Nicola Dordoni, Renaissance ceiling frescoes and an entrance portal by Gio Ponti. Meissen's historic porcelain, first produced in the German region of Saxony in the early 18th century, is displayed alongside more contemporary product lines, such as fine jewellery and Meissen Home, a range of furnishings inspired by designs held in the company's archives. The products are arranged across eight themed rooms.
Via Montenapoleone 3, T 02 8942 3725, www.meissen.com

ESCAPES

WHERE TO GO IF YOU WANT TO LEAVE TOWN

The Milanese take full advantage of the city's proximity to the Alps and the coast, and many spend almost every weekend out of town. The lakes offer the quickest escape. Como (opposite) is a 50-minute journey; Lugano, over the Swiss border, is an hour away; and it's two hours to Garda. All are accessible by train. Also within striking distance are Bergamo (see p102) and Modena, for chef Massimo Bottura's divine Osteria Francescana (Via Stella 22, T 05 922 3912). Further afield, journey times to Rome have been halved by the high-speed Frecciarossa train, which travels to the capital in less than three hours, or to Bologna (overleaf) in just one.

For a dip in the Med, the Portofino promontory is an enchanting destination, a marine park boasting forested trails and crystalline waters that cosies up to the village's famous harbour. Nearby is the bay of Paraggi and one of the area's few public beaches, Bagni Fiore (Via Paraggi a Mare 1, Santa Margherita, T 01 8528 4831), and Camogli, where the Fondazione Pier Luigi e Natalina Remotti (Via Castagneto 52, T 01 8577 2137) is a fascinating modern art space in a deconsecrated church. From Milan, it takes two hours by train. Alternatively, head to a mountain spa like Therme Vals (see p100) or, in South Tyrol, Vigilius Resort (Vigiljoch, Lana, T 04 7355 6600) and Terme Merano (Piazza Terme 9, Merano, T 04 7325 2000). To visit either, catch a train to Bolzano, then it's a 40km taxi ride. *For full addresses, see Resources.*

Casa sull'Albero, Lake Como

This 2013 hotel on the eastern side of Lake Como was the brainchild of architect Giorgio Melesi. The spectacular setting was a key influence on the design, and each of the 12 rooms and suites has a transparent glass wall to make the most of the view. The materials draw on the surrounding environment too: local stone and wood feature in both the exterior construction and the interiors. There's a heated outdoor pool, a mini-spa with massage area and gym, a cinema room and a good library stocked with books on art and photography. The hotel is just across the water from the restaurants and bars of Lecco, but with Casa sull'Albero's sylvan charms at your disposal, you may not feel the need to travel that far.
Viale Penati 5-7, Malgrate,
T 03 411 880 440, www.casa-sullalbero.it

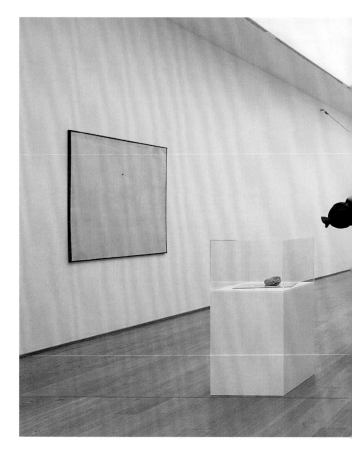

MAMbo, Bologna

Don't be disheartened by the porticoed exterior – the Museo d'Arte Moderna di Bologna (MAMbo) is every inch a modern temple to the cutting edge. Permanent collections document major movements of the 20th- and 21st-century, such as Arte Povera, shaped by the work of Pier Paolo Calzolari, Giulio Paolini and Gilberto Zorio, and influencing the oeuvre of Hidetoshi Nagasawa and Eliseo Mattiacci (all above).

Although there's a commitment to Italian artists, a number of recent acquisitions have locked into global trends, from the multi-faceted pieces of American Matthew Day Jackson to a Le Corbusier-inspired collage by the Bulgarian Plamen Dejanoff. Bologna itself is a delight, boasting some of the country's finest medieval architecture.
Via Don Minzoni 14, T 051 649 6611, www.mambo-bologna.org

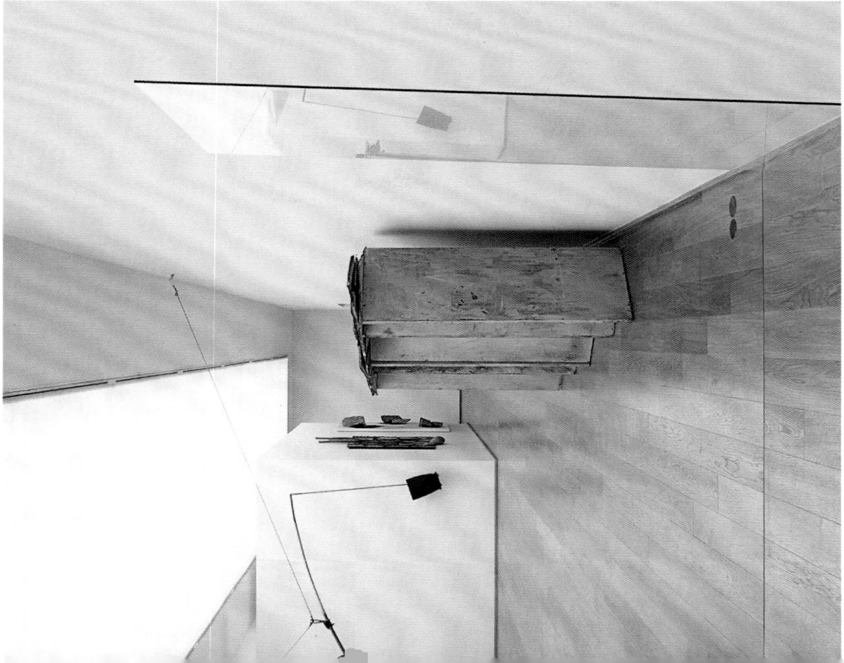

Therme Vals, Vals, Switzerland

Milan's proximity to Switzerland means that Therme Vals makes for a pleasant three-and-a-half-hour car ride. Here, Peter Zumthor has used 60,000 slabs of Valser quartzite to create a cathedral to bathing, with indoor and outdoor thermal pools. The use of light and shade, and open and enclosed spaces, enhances the feeling of wellbeing as you take in the health benefits of the spring. Book in advance for the wellness centre, which offers a range of treatments, from masks and exfoliation to wraps and massage. Stay at the interconnected 7132 Hotel (spa entry included), choosing one of the new Kengo Kuma-designed oak cocoons, or at the excellent family guesthouse Hotel Alpina (T +41 819 207 040), where you should reserve a modernised room. *T +41 587 132 000, www.7132.ch*

GombitHotel, Bergamo

In the foothills of the Alps, clasped within defensive walls, Bergamo's old town has retained its medieval and 16th-century outline. A backdrop of mountains, valleys and plains make it easy to forget you're only 50 minutes from central Milan as you meander through the ancient site. Built flush against the 13th-century stone Torre del Gombito, the Gombit is the first design hotel within the walls of the *città* *alta* (upper city). The 13 rooms, which have interiors designed by Gio Pozzi, are all unique but share a minimal aesthetic (Suite 14, above). More than just a place to sleep, Gombit functions as an experimental gallery, where young creatives can display their work, adding an artistic feel to public spaces such as the study area (opposite). *Via Mario Lupo 6, T 03 524 7009,* *www.gombithotel.it*

NOTES

SKETCHES AND MEMOS